Language Arts Crossword Puzzles

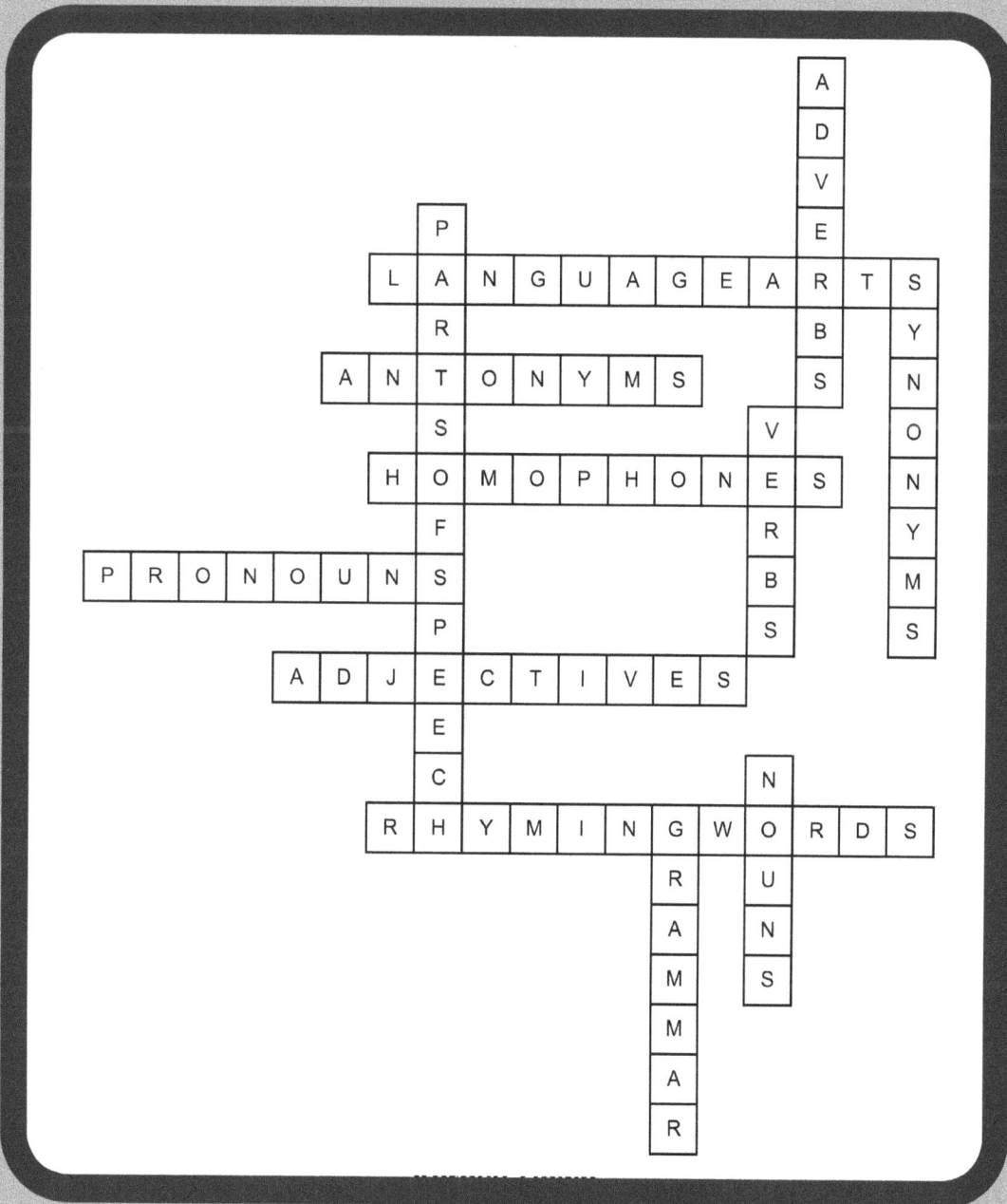

Grades 1–4

Written by Rebecca Stark

ISBN 978-1-56644-567-2

Educational Books 'n' Bingo

Printed in the United States of America.

TABLE OF CONTENTS

*An alphabetical list of possible answers from which to choose is provided for each crossword puzzle. Use these lists at your discretion.

Synonyms

Change the word shown in **bold** with a synonym.

> **Example:** The waiter brought a **large** piece of cake.

> If it fits, you might want to try **"huge."**

ACROSS

3   I ate a **tiny** piece of pie.

4   The story was about an **evil** witch.

8   I made my mother a **present** for Mother's Day.

10   The two shirts were **alike.**

12   Mom **shouted** for me to come home.

13   I tried not to **giggle** when I saw the funny hat.

15   My **dad** left work early so he could come to my baseball game.

18   Dora was **ill,** so she stayed home from school.

19   The movie was about to **begin.**

DOWN

1   The clothes in the dryer are still **wet.**

2   Mom asked me to **shut** the door.

5   Her answer was **right.**

6   The child's clothes were **dirty** after playing in the mud.

7   Barbara was **weary** after studying for hours.

8   Stephanie was **happy** that her friend was visiting.

9   The runner was very **quick.**

11   Jane wants to go to the movies. I want to go **too.**

14   Mother placed a paper doily **below** the cake.

16   Kim was **mad** that she was not invited.

17   The family that moved next door is very **wealthy.**

19   The babysitter read a funny **tale** to the child.

          Language Arts Crossword Puzzles: Grades 1–4

Synonyms

5 Language Arts Crossword Puzzles: Grades 1–4

Antonyms

Change the word shown in **bold** with an antonym.

Example: The waiter brought a **large** piece of cake.

If it fits, you might want to try **small.**

ACROSS

2   I looked and saw that it was **light** outside.

4   Keith's brother tried to **break** his toy.

5   Sam's room was very **tidy.**

7   Jack went **under** the rope barrier.

9   Laura **lost** the tennis match

10 Ella prefers to play **inside.**

11 Jennifer arrived at her appointment **late.**

13 Wendy was very **rude** to others.

16 The movie was **ending.**

18 Peter hopes to **sell** the red bicycle.

DOWN

1   Becca **loves** spaghetti and meatballs.

3   The path was very **narrow.**

6   The **old** man entered the store.

8   The boy entered the room **loudly.**

9   The clothes in the dryer are **dry.**

12 Jim **always** watches the news at night.

13 The directions on the door said to **push.**

14 Kim asked where the **entrance** was.

15 I **lost** my wallet in the ice cream shop.

16 The boy walked **quickly** towards his house.

17 Jeff was **pleased** that his uninvited friend came to the party.

Antonyms

Parts of Speech

ACROSS

3   Adverb in the sentence "Zack walked quickly down the hall."

4   *A, an* and *the*

7   Describes a noun or pronoun

8   Adjective in the sentence "Sophie bought a red dress in the mall."

9   Links a noun, pronoun or phrase to other words; *to* or *of,* for example

10   Pronoun that might take the place of "He and Rebecca"

11   Pronoun meaning "you and I"

13   Describes or shows an action

14   Joins words or groups of words

16   *Book* is the ___ form of the noun

18   Acts like a noun

DOWN

1   *Mary* is this type of noun

2   *Books* is the ___ form of the noun

5   Another word for an exclamation

6   Names a person, place, or thing

7   Describes a verb, an adjective or another___

12   *Girl* is this type of noun

15   Preposition in the sentence "I am going to the store."

17   Verb in the sentence "I read two books last week."

19   Interjection in the sentence "Ouch! That hurt!"

Parts of Speech

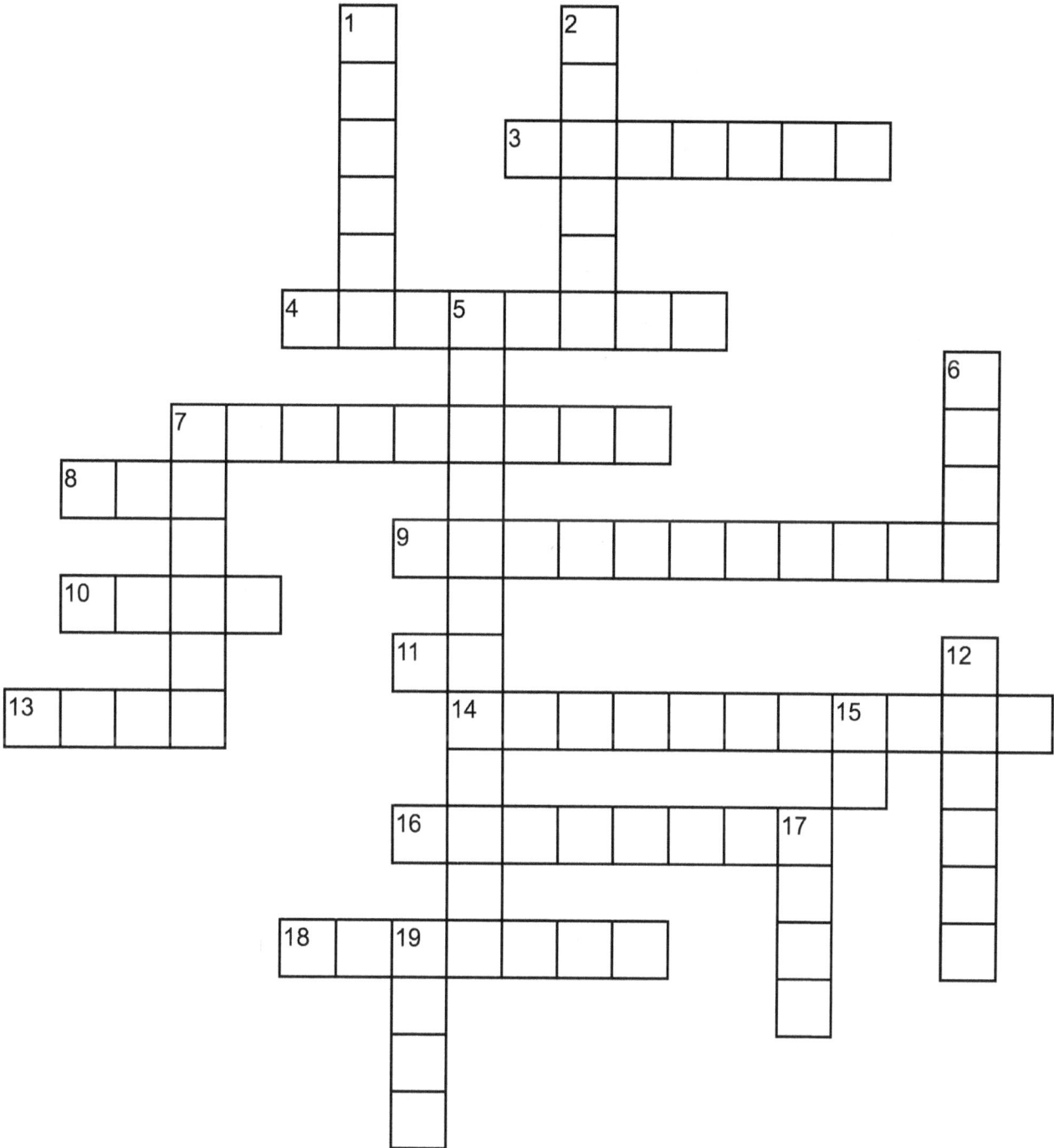

Rhyming Words

ACROSS

5   Brought to an end; rhymes with *won*

6   Humorous; rhymes with *bunny*

7   Before the present time; rhymes with *last*

10   A system of rules that must be followed; rhymes with *jaw*

11   Antonym for *false*; rhymes with *blue*

12   Upper layer of earth; rhymes with *soil*

13   A synonym for *yell;* rhymes with *dream*

16   A colored substance spread over a surface; rhymes with *faint*

19   Seashells are often found here; rhymes with *more*

20   Synonym for *throw;* rhymes with *loss*

21   Antonym of *far;* rhymes with *hear*

DOWN

1   Park with animals; rhymes with *too*

2   A present; rhymes with *shift*

3   Past tense of keep; rhymes with *wept*

4   Equal to 100 pennies; rhymes with *collar*

5   Just before sunrise; rhymes with *lawn*

8   A homonym for *sale;* rhymes with *pail*

9   Tells an untruth; rhymes with *tries*

14   What a baby does when hungry; rhymes with *dries*

15   A rodent; rhymes with *house*

17   Antonym of *thin;* rhymes with *trick*

18   A large, heavy mammal; rhymes with *wear*

Rhyming Words

Nouns: At School

ACROSS

2   A group of students who meet regularly

4   You might learn about circles and squares in this class

5   A short test

8   You might learn about clouds in this class

12 The person in charge of a school

16 Tasks to do after school

17 Something you write with if you want to be able to erase

18 What the children in a classroom are called

21 What you get from the library

22 A drawing of all or part of Earth's surface

23 You play sports in this part of the school; short form

DOWN

1   A piece of furniture similar to a table

2   What the students in a class usually sit on

3   This person might help you if you scrape your knee

6   Something you write with for your final copy

7   This person is in charge of the library

9   The leader of a classroom

10 Something you write on

11 What children get in the cafeteria

13 Soft substance used for writing

14 A book with words and their definitions

15 It rings when classes are over

19 A device used to remove chalk or other markings

20 A set of questions to determine knowledge

21 Some children ride on one to get to school

Nouns: At School

© Barbara M. Peller   Language Arts Crossword Puzzles: Grades 1–4

Nouns: At Home

ACROSS

2 A floor covering

5 Tool used to smooth clothing and other items

6 Tells us the time

8 Covering made of cloth to keep you warm

12 What we eat

13 Utensil with prongs for lifting food

14 A piece of furniture with a flat top and one or more legs

16 Sharp instrument with blade for cutting

18 You probably rest your head on this when you sleep

19 Animal kept in home for pleasure

DOWN

1 A round, open-top container

3 Where a car is sometimes kept

4 The one in the kitchen is sometimes used to wash dishes

7 We sit on them around the kitchen table

8 Furniture to sleep on

9 Room where an oven is found

10 Electrical device for making toast

11 At the entrance to a building, room, or vehicle

13 A group consisting of parents and children living together

15 Device for giving light

17 Furniture for several people to sit on

20 Short for "television"

Nouns: At Home

Language Arts Crossword Puzzles: Grades 1–4

Pronouns

Fill in each blank with a pronoun.

Use context clues to help you decide which pronoun to use.

ACROSS

2 Emma thanked me when I gave ___ some of my popcorn.

3 When the phone rang, Mom asked me to answer ___.

5 I pointed to a book at the end of the table and said, "Please pass me ___ book."

7 I was giving out cake to the guests, and Hannah said to put ___ on the table.

9 Jake likes steak, but ___ doesn't like fish.

10 We put our gifts on the floor, but Sean and Kelly put ___ on the table.

12 I asked my mother to take ___ to the mall so I could meet my friends.

13 The guard asked for our tickets. I gave him ___ and Juan gave him his.

14 Jessie's mom handed Jessie her ticket and said, "Here, this one is ___."

17 Jim thanked me when I gave ___ some of my candy.

18 Jess and I like seals, so ___ decided to work together on our science project.

DOWN

1 I picked a book and said, "I choose ___ one."

4 John said, "These shoes fit better than ___," pointing to the ones on the floor.

6 I handed two books to the librarian and said, "I would like to take out ___ books."

8 I showed the librarian the books and asked her where to put ___.

10 Josh and Manuel often did ___ homework together.

11 Martin and ___ went to the store because we needed glue.

15 We usually ride ___ bikes to school.

16 Mary likes biographies, but ___ doesn't like mysteries.

Clara Barton

Pronouns

Language Arts Crossword Puzzles: Grades 1–4

Verbs

Fill in the correct form of the verb in parentheses.

Use context clues to help. Some answers require two words.

ACROSS

1   Nick (fall) in the playground and hurt his knee.

6   Keith (run) down the street quickly because he was late for the bus.

7   Mom (arrange) the flowers in the vase before she put them on the table.

9   I like to ride in the front seat, but yesterday I (ride) in the back.

10 "I (eat) lunch later," Melissa explained.

11 The family (adopt) a dog from the rescue shelter yesterday.

14 The students (eat) in the museum's cafe during yesterday's field trip.

16 Keith (sleep) in the top bunk when he went to camp.

18 Three girls and four boys (come) to my birthday party last week.

19 I (think) it was going to rain, but I was wrong.

21 Kathy always (sit) in the front of the class so she can see the board.

22 The teacher (say) that we should open our books to page 100.

DOWN

1   Nikki (forget) to sign the check, so the clerk handed it back to her.

2   My class (read) that book last year.

3   I (know) all the answers to the questions on the test yesterday.

4   Dad told me to (call) him when I got to my friend's house.

5   Katie (do) her homework early last night so she could watch TV.

7   We (go) to the movies and then we are having lunch in the park.

8   Sue (drink) several glasses of water every day.

12 I already (drink) two glasses of water today.

13 Fran, Mindy, and Sarah (go) to the movies last Saturday.

15 Jackie (eat) lunch in the cafeteria, but Sue and Jeff go home for lunch.

17 "Look! I (find) a dollar bill in the playground!" Missy shouted.

20 I have three coats, but my brother (have) four.

21 Mark, Sam, and Dave always (sit) in the front row of the movie theater.

22 Rich (see) the crossing guard's sign, so he stopped.

   Language Arts Crossword Puzzles: Grades 1–4

Verbs

Language Arts Crossword Puzzles: Grades 1–4

Adjectives

Fill in the blanks so that the two sets of analogies have the same relationship.

Examples: (The relationship is shown in parentheses.)

big : large :: rich : wealthy (synonyms)

big : little :: large : small   (antonyms)

high : higher :: small :: smaller   (degree)

ACROSS

1 ___ : strong :: sick : healthy

3 wet :___ :: kind : mean

6 busy : busiest :: happy : ___

8 ___ : dull :: happy : sad

9 smart : smarter : soft : ___

10 ___ : clumsy :: easy : difficult

11 lucky : ___ : tall : taller

13 ___ : worse :: good : better

14 thick : ___ :: long ; longest

16 pretty : ___ :: little : tiny

DOWN

1 good : best :: warm : ___

2 ___ : wet :: large : huge

4 alike : ___ :: true : false

5 relaxed : ___ :: rich : poor

7 angry : ___ :: hungry : hungrier

11 cloudy : sunny :: quiet : ___

12 hot : ___ :: thick : thin

13 good : ___ :: long : longer

15 ___ : stormy :: pleased : angry

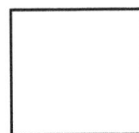

small   smaller   smalllest

Adjectives

big

bigger

biggest

Language Arts Crossword Puzzles: Grades 1–4

Adverbs

Identify the adverb in each sentence to solve the crossword.

ACROSS

3   Kim was waiting on line since 8 am.

6   Sam shouted loudly to his brother.

7   Katie never walks in the road.

9   Zack was really hungry, so he ordered two hamburgers.

12   The rabbit magically appeared.

13   Stacy's grandma waited patiently for her to exit the school.

15   The girl politely asked her teacher for another sheet of paper.

17   Bob angrily slammed the door.

18   Becca happily agreed to do the dishes.

19   The child waited eagerly for his turn on the slide.

20   Liz read quietly in the library.

22   It is almost noon.

23   Rick got in trouble for acting badly in class.

DOWN

1   I sometimes empty the dishwasher.

2   The children played nicely.

4   The teacher clearly explained the lesson.

5   Sara bravely confronted the bully.

8   My dad drives his motorcycle safely.

10   Jack always eat cereal for breakfast.

11   Sean carefully opened the package.

14   Josh finally finished her homework.

16   Our class trip to the zoo is tomorrow.

21   I arrived at the doctor's office early.

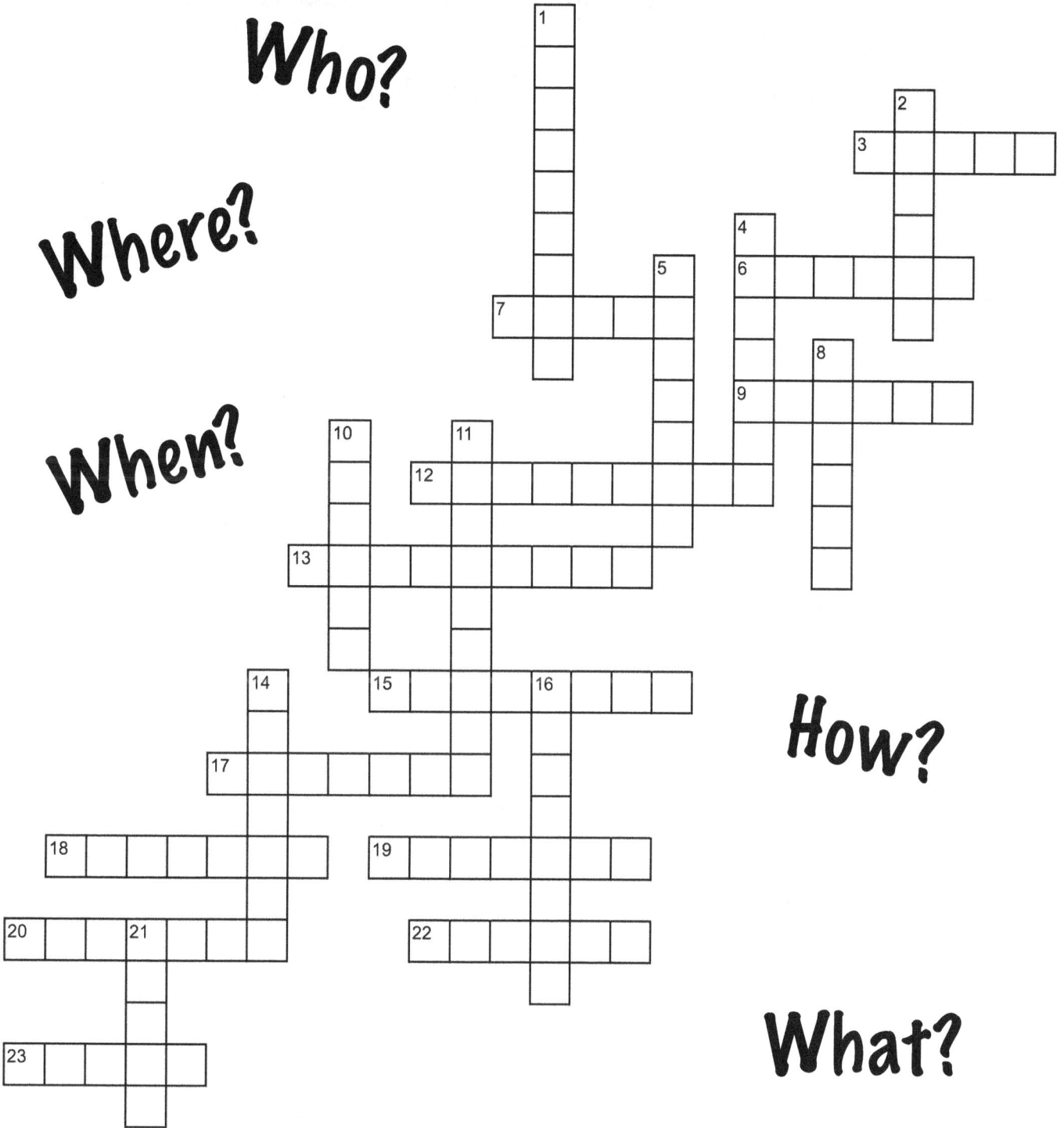

Adverbs

Who?

Where?

When?

How?

What?

How Often?

People in Our Lives Word Search

```
E R M O T H E R O A E X V Z P I
N E S R U N G Q M R S I S T E R
B A D H M H E D P E U J Y E A P
M V Z L E E N X X H K V B B O S
R R M L A A T S I T N E D L N B
Q B C Q R P M T B O F D I J I E
G N M G R J I S E R Q C A V S A
U U C E B E T C H B E B J M U N
T X B Q H E H P N O F Z L R O A
B M H C A O C T F I O Z U E C I
Y V G C A K G F A Y R C D X Y R
E D H Y B U I Z J F E P C E N A
S E E D C C N D N E I R F Y C R
R H V L E L X T R H I O W L P B
M D Q R K O D X D O C T O R W I
O I T G R A N D P A W J O N V L
```

FAMILY MEMBERS

AUNT
BROTHER
COUSIN
FATHER
GRANDMA
GRANDPA
MOTHER
SISTER
UNCLE

OTHERS

COACH
DENTIST
DOCTOR
FRIEND
LIBRARIAN 1
NURSE
POLICE OFFICER
PRINCIPAL
TEACHER

Language Arts Crossword Puzzles: Grades 1–4

Sounds the Same! Different Meanings!

Underline the letter in front of each correct answer.

1. It was a very cloudy ___.
   G. knight
   H. night

2. The ___ was hired to clean the room.
   N. made
   O. maid

3. There is a ___ in the shoelace.
   L. not
   M. knot

4. Kelly dressed as a ___ for Halloween.
   O. witch
   P. which

5. I ___ the song of the ice cream truck.
   O. here
   P. hear

6. Jennifer ___ her tennis match.
   G. one
   H. won

7. Dave ate a ___ for dessert.
   O. pear
   P. pair

8. My mother bought two dresses at the ___.
   M. sail
   N. sale

9. The ___ was good for playing baseball.
   E. weather
   F. whether

10. Sara is going on vacation next ___.
    S. week
    T. weak

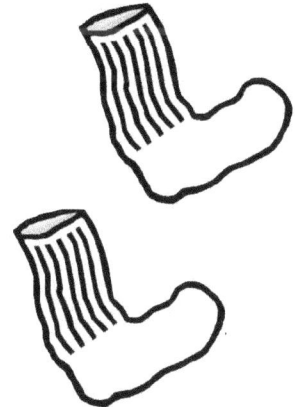

The underlined letters will describe these words!

Language Arts Crossword Puzzles: Grades 1–4

Hidden Pets

Find the pet hiding in each sentence.

1. If I share my chips, will you share your cookies?

PET: _____

2. They do good work when they try.

PET: _____

3. Stand up on your toes.

PET: _____

4. Eric ate three pieces of pie.

PET: _____

5. Sam asked if Roger wanted to come to his party.

PET: _____

6. I ate ham, Sterling ate chicken, and Seth ate pork.

PET: _____

7. The teacher explained to Kip, "Igneous rocks include obsidian and basalt."

PET: _____

8. Keep up the good work.

PET: _____

               Science Crossword Puzzles: Grades 6 & Up

Solutions*

*Optional Lists of Answers

Alphabetical lists of the answers are provided. These may be used to help solve the puzzle from the beginning, to assist those having difficulty, or not at all.

Synonyms

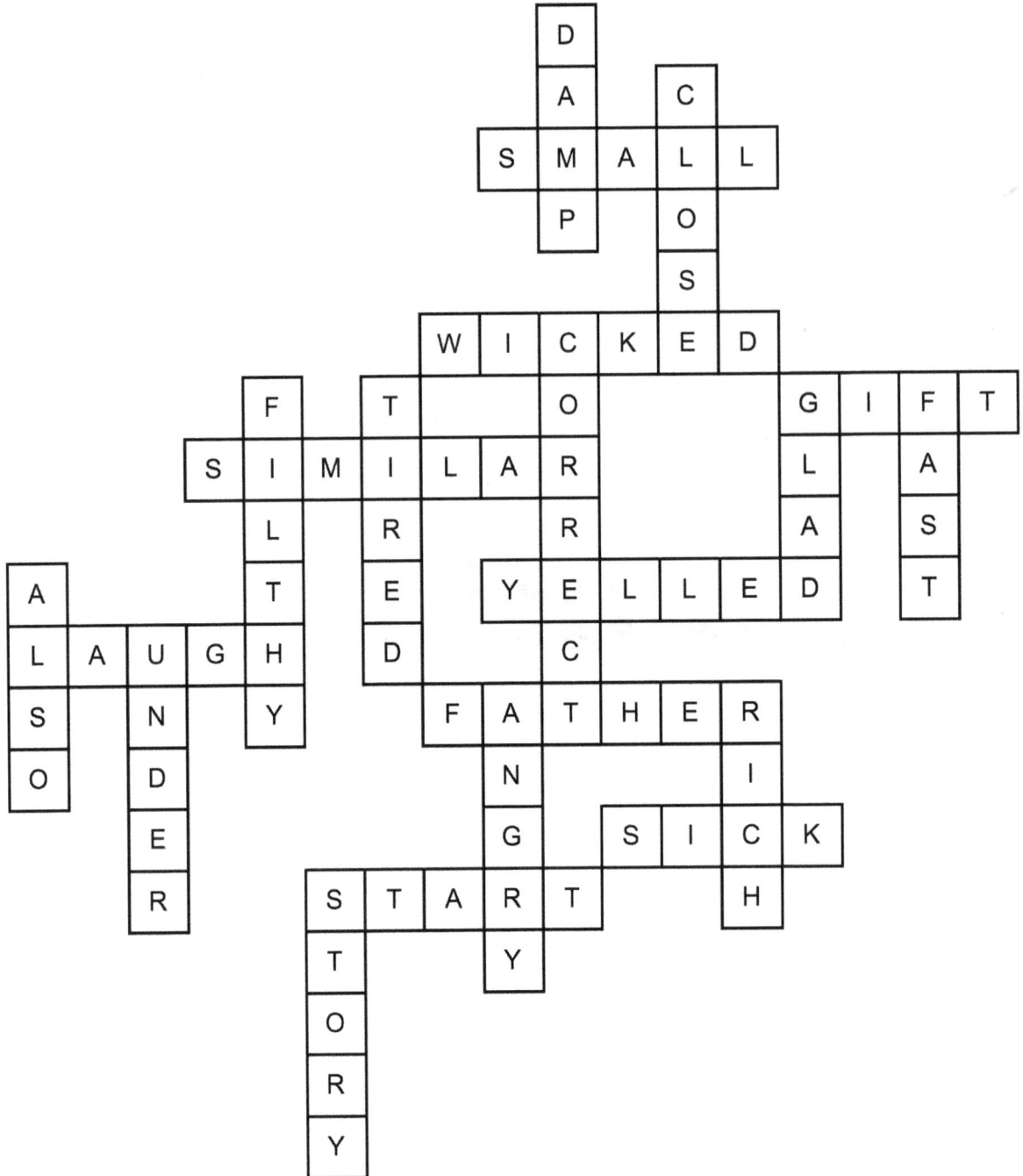

Antonyms

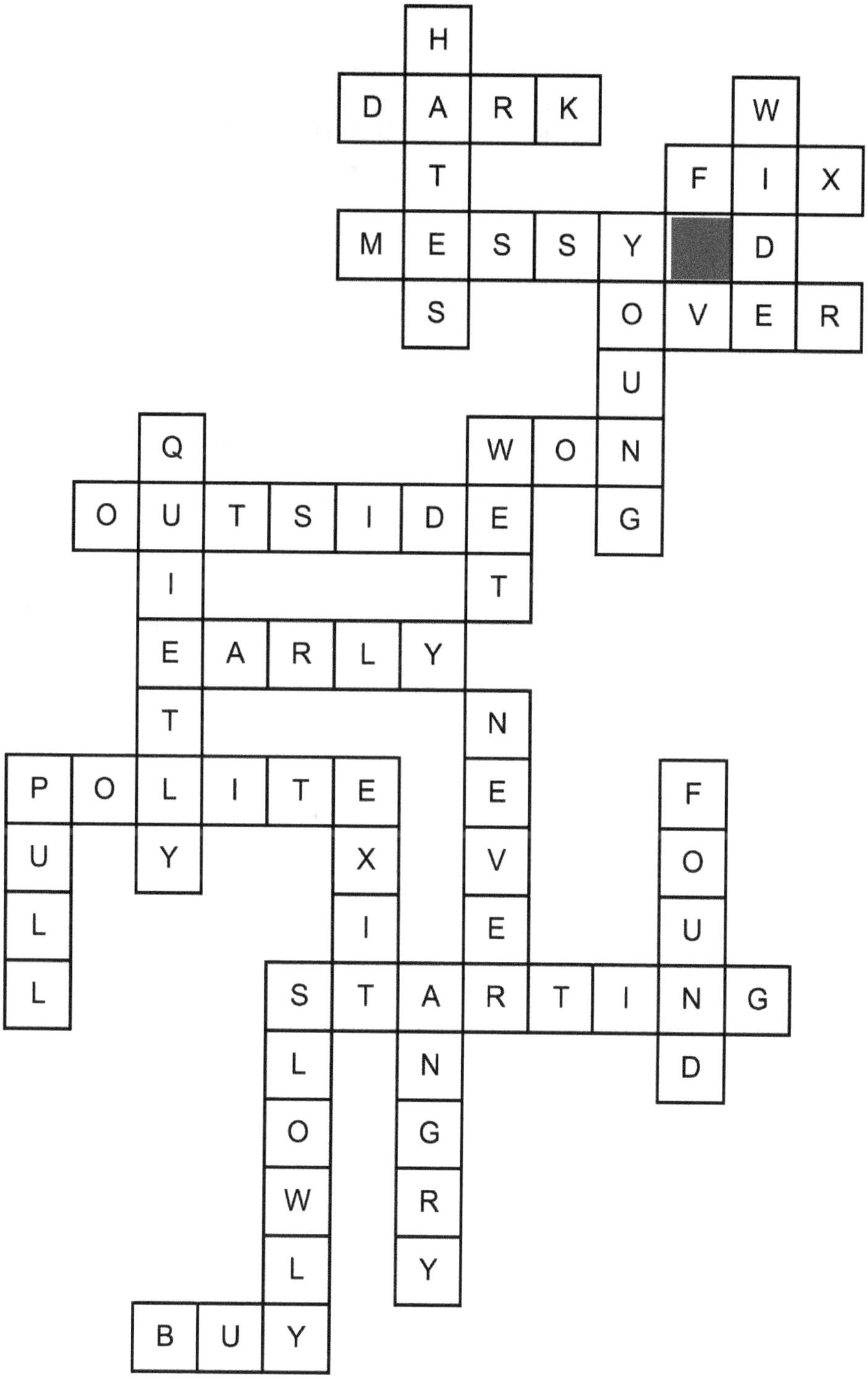
HATES
DARK
WIDE
FIX
MESSY
OVER
YOUNG
WON
QUIETLY
OUTSIDE
WET
EARLY
NEVER
POLITE
PULL
EXIT
FOUND
STARTING
SLOWLY
ANGRY
BUY

Parts of Speech

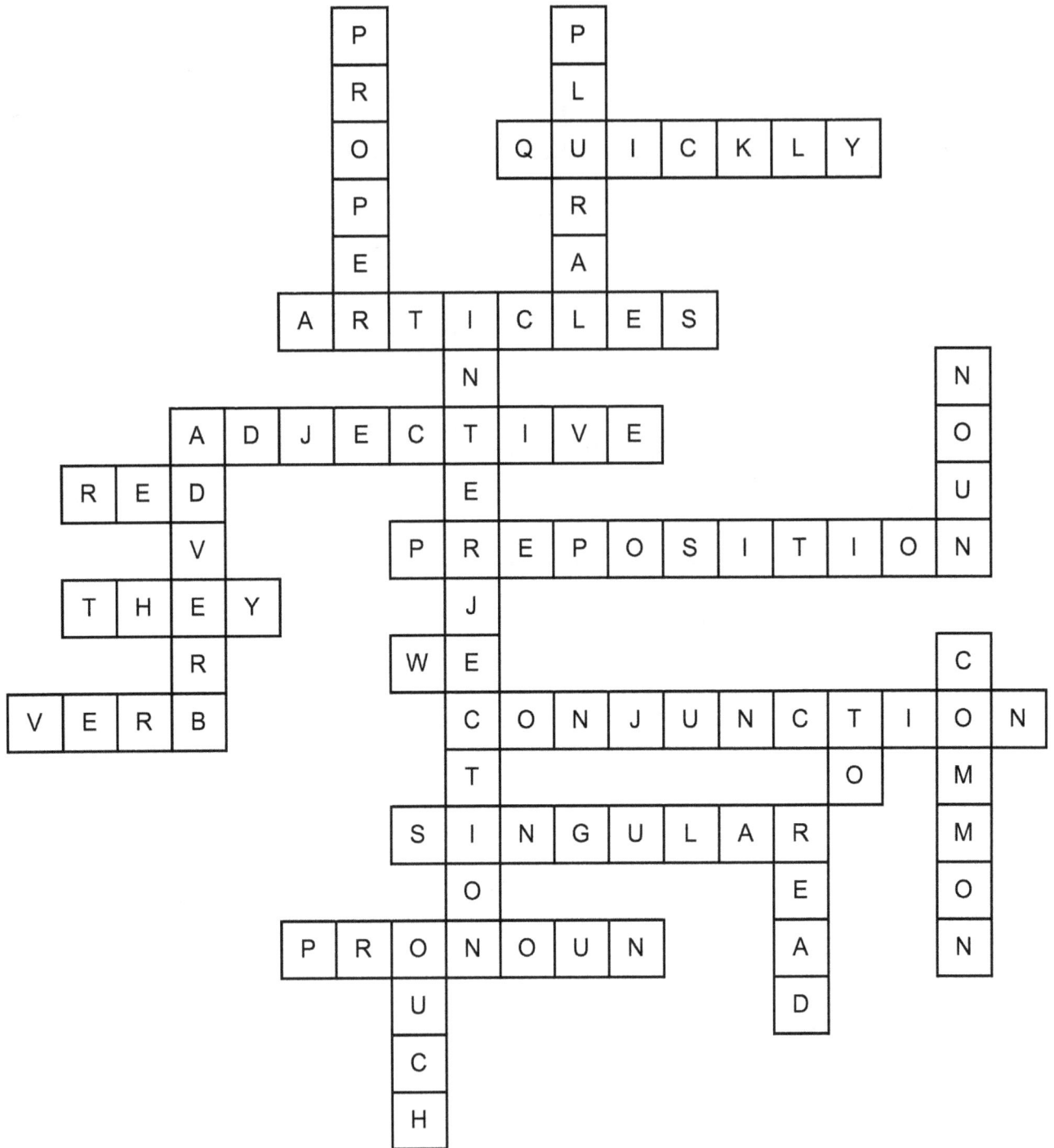

P
R
O
P
E
A R T I C L E S
          N

P
L
Q U I C K L Y
U
R
A

        A D J E C T I V E
R E D
      V
T H E Y
      R
V E R B

N
O
U
                    P R E P O S I T I O N
                    J
                    W E
                    C O N J U N C T I O N
                    T   O
                    S I N G U L A R
                    O   E
        P R O N O U N   A
                    U   D
                    C
                    H

C
O
M
M
O
N

Rhyming Words

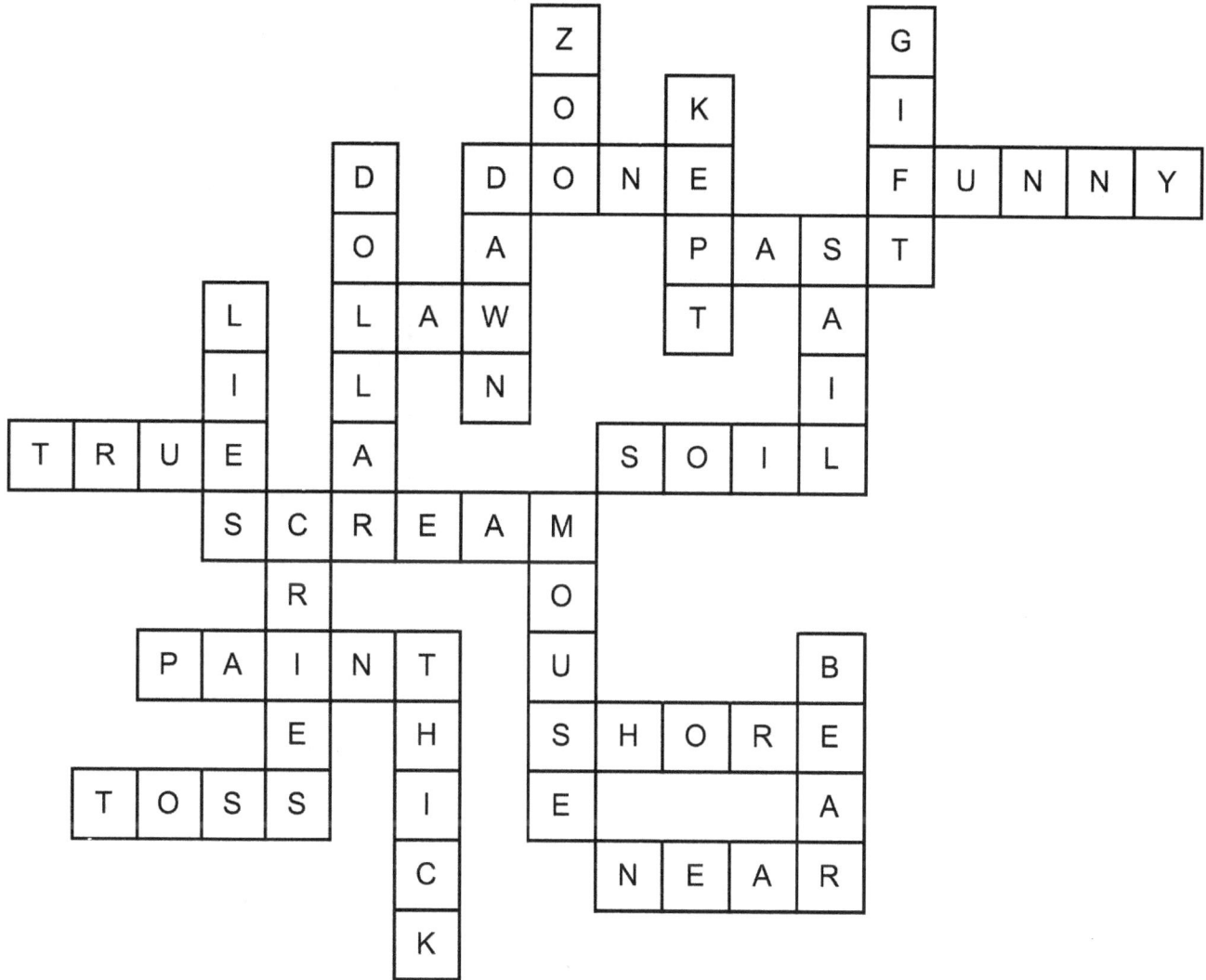

A crossword puzzle grid with the following filled-in letters:

- FUNNY (across)
- DONE (across)
- PAST (across)
- LAWN (across)
- TRUE (across)
- SOIL (across)
- SCREAM (across)
- PAINT (across)
- SHORE (across)
- TOSS (across)
- NEAR (across)

Vertical words and letters include:
- ZONE
- GIFT
- DOLLA
- KEPT
- STAIL
- LILAS
- CREAM
- MOUSE
- THICK
- BEAR
- PEN

Language Arts Crossword Puzzles: Grades 1–4

Nouns: At School

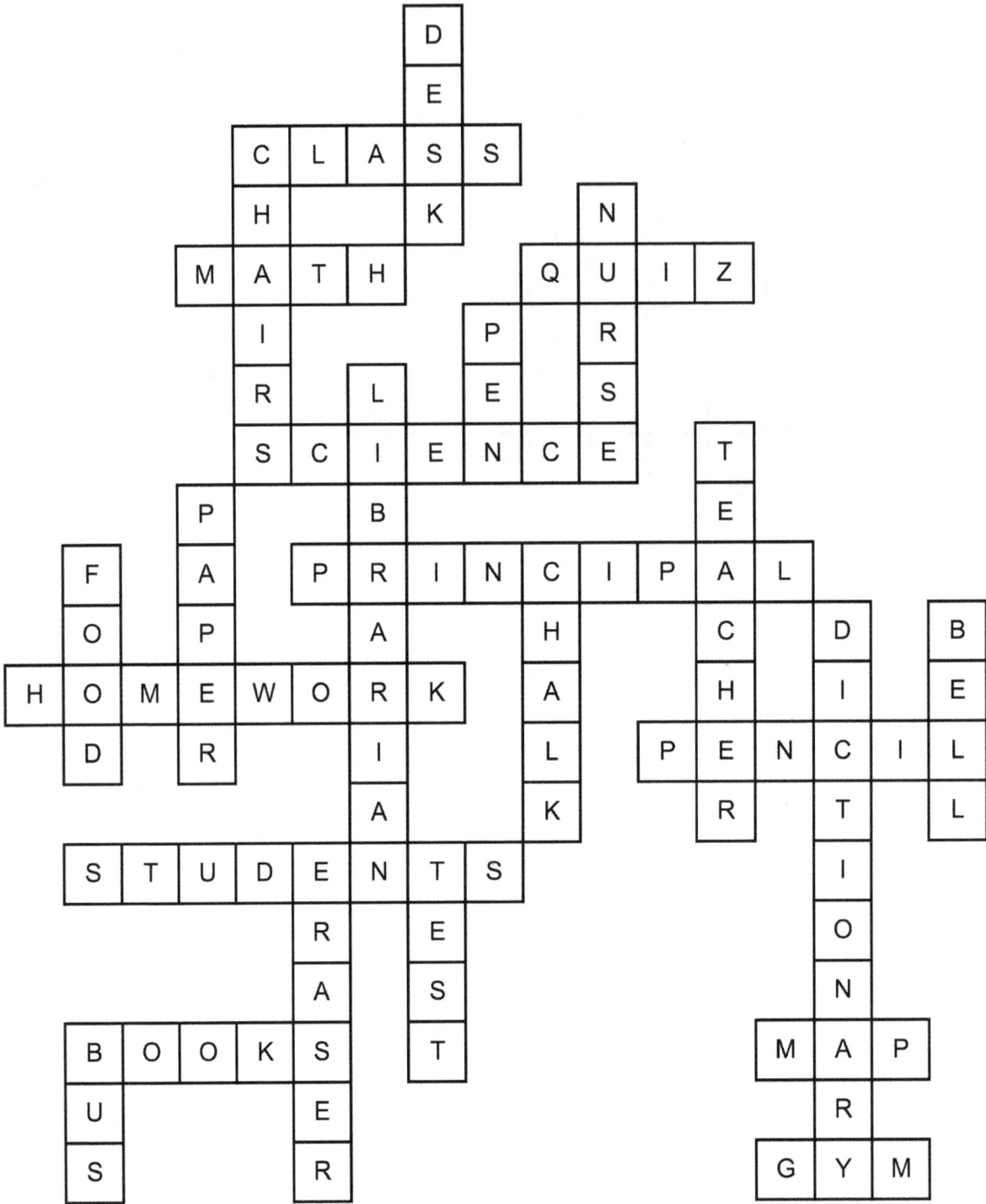

A crossword puzzle with the following words filled in:

DESK, CLASS, CHAIR, MATH, HAIR, SCIENCE, QUIZ, NURSE, PAPER, PAGE, PRINCIPAL, TEACHER, FOOD, HOMEWORK, PENCIL, BELL, STUDENTS, LIBRARIAN, BRAIN, HALLWALK, BUS, BOOKS, ERASER, RESTT, MAP, GYM, ADDITION

Across answers: CLASS, MATH, QUIZ, SCIENCE, PRINCIPAL, HOMEWORK, PENCIL, STUDENTS, BOOKS, MAP, GYM

Down answers: DESK, CHAIR, HAIR, NURSE, PAPER, PAGE, FOOD, TEACHER, ADDITION, BELL, LIBRARIAN, BRAIN, HALLWALK, RESTT, ERASER, BUS

Nouns: At Home

Pronouns

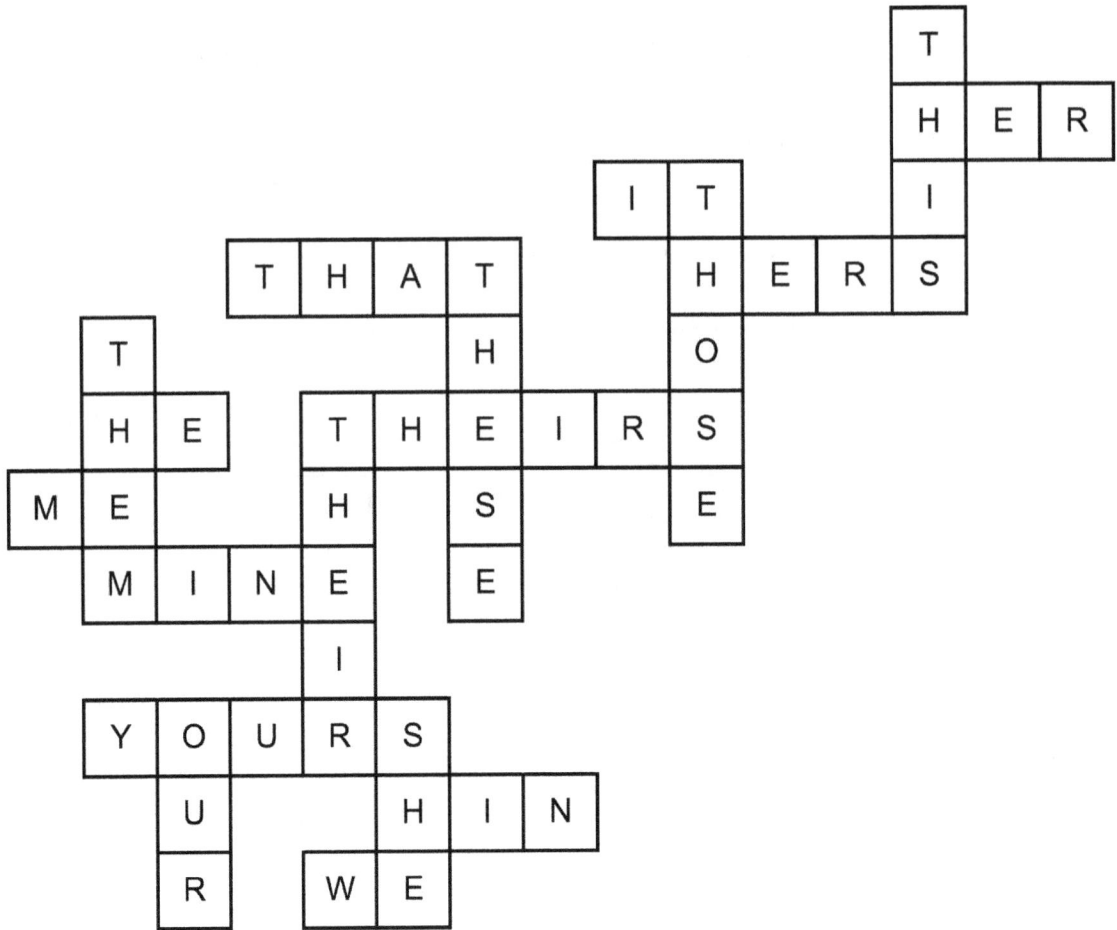

A crossword puzzle grid containing the following pronouns:

Across and down entries spell: THEIR, IT, HER, THIS, THAT, HERS, THOSE, THE, THEIRS, THESE, ME, HE, MINE, THEIR, YOURS, YOUR, HIM, HIN, WE

Verbs

Adjectives

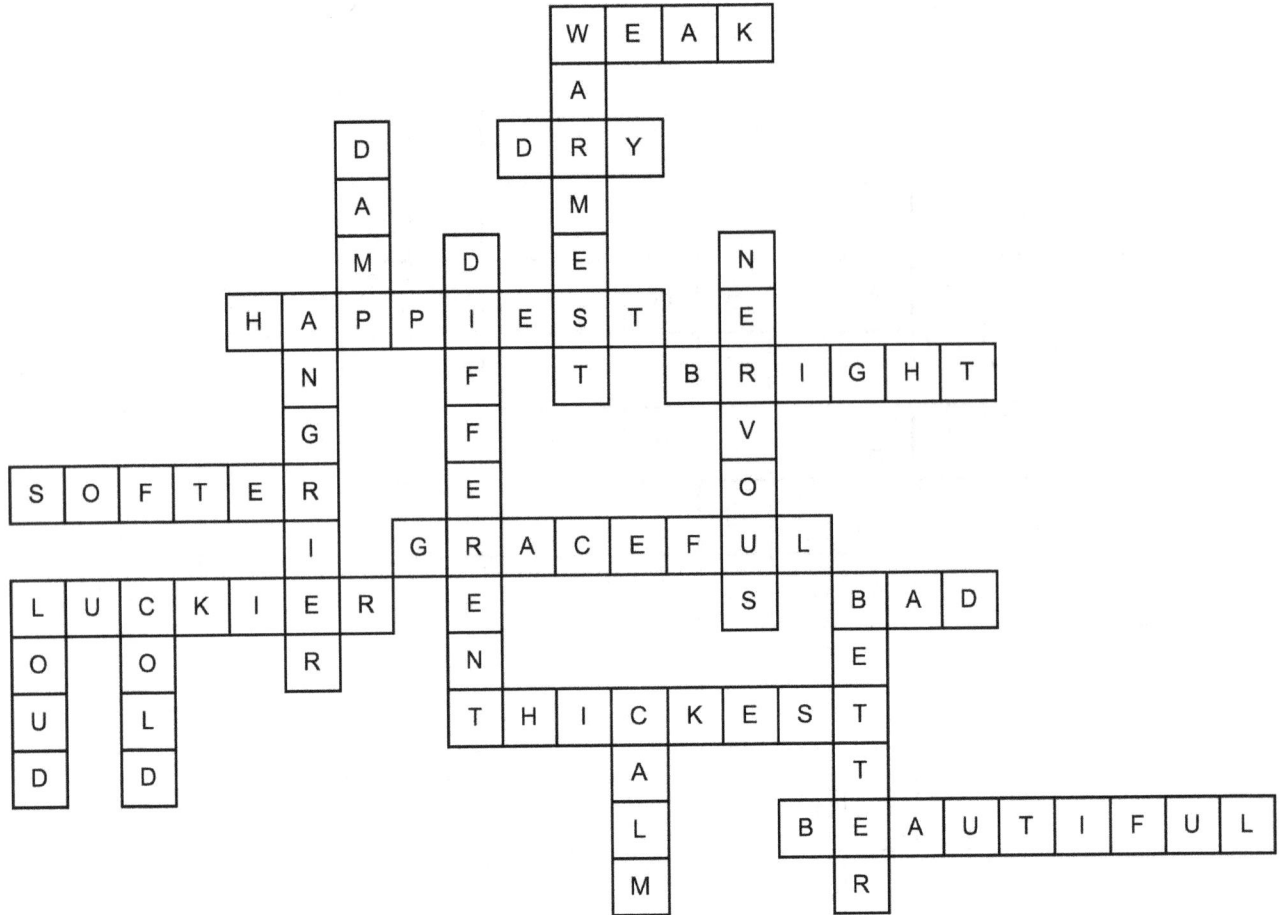

Language Arts Crossword Puzzles: Grades 1–4

Adverbs

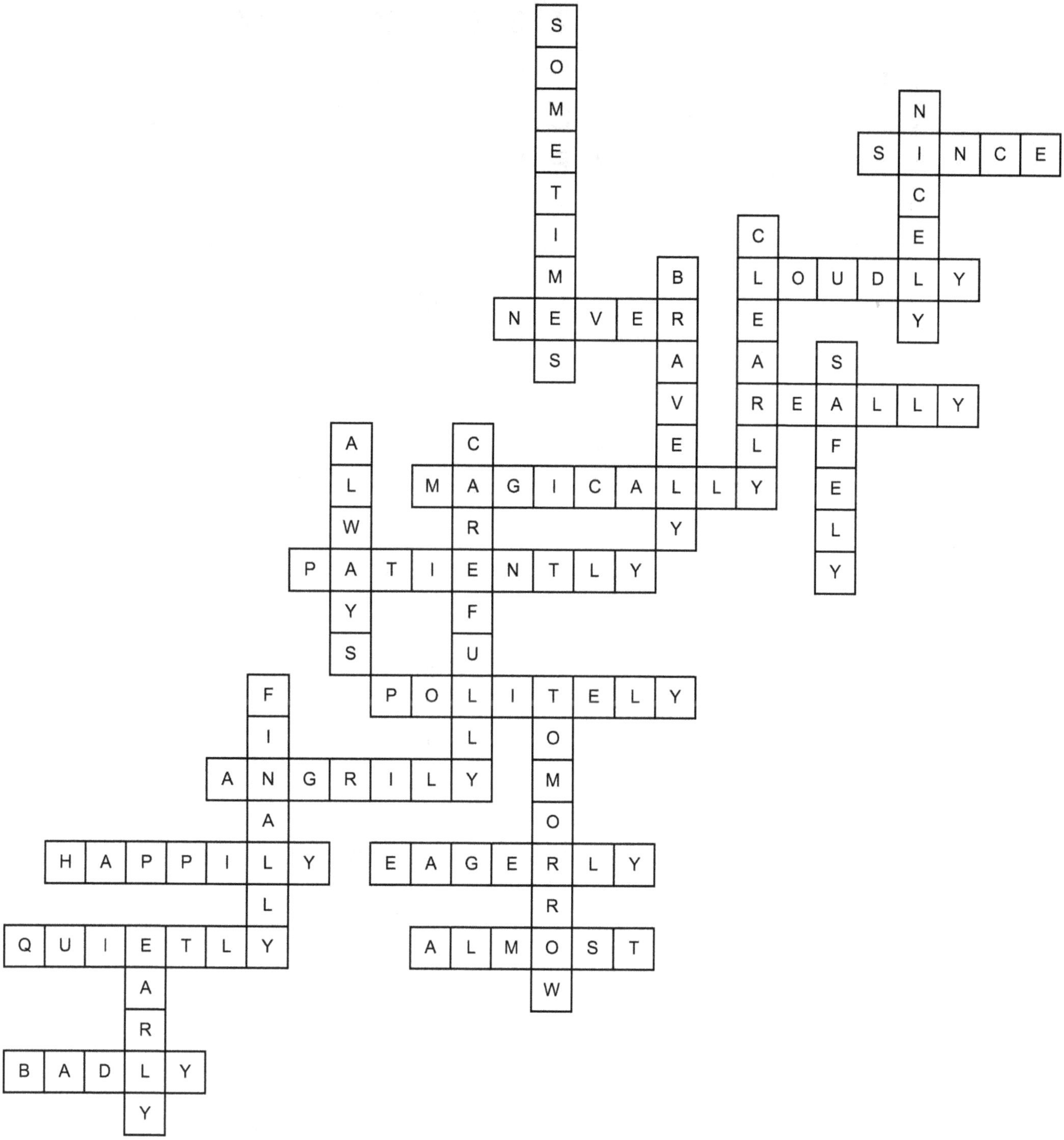
SOMETIMES
NICELY
SINCE
CLEARLY
LOUDLY
BRAVELY
NEVER
SAFELY
REALLY
ALWAYS
CAREFULLY
MAGICALLY
PATIENTLY
POLITELY
FINALLY
TOMORROW
ANGRILY
HAPPILY
EAGERLY
QUIETLY
ALMOST
EARLY
BADLY

People in Our Lives Word Search

	1	2	3	4	5	6	7	8	9	10	11	12	13	14	15	16
1	E	R	M	O	T	H	E	R	O	A	E	X	V	Z	P	I
2	N	E	S	R	U	N	G	Q	M	R	S	I	S	T	E	R
3	B	A	D	H	M	H	E	D	P	E	U	J	Y	E	A	P
4	M	V	Z	L	E	E	N	X	X	H	K	V	B	B	O	S
5	R	R	M	L	A	A	T	S	I	T	N	E	D	L	N	B
6	Q	B	C	Q	R	P	M	T	B	O	F	D	I	J	I	E
7	G	N	M	G	R	J	I	S	E	R	Q	C	A	V	S	A
8	U	U	C	E	B	E	T	C	H	B	E	B	J	M	U	N
9	T	X	B	Q	H	E	H	P	N	O	F	Z	L	R	O	A
10	B	M	H	C	A	O	C	T	F	I	O	Z	U	E	C	I
11	Y	V	G	C	A	K	G	F	A	Y	R	C	D	X	Y	R
12	E	D	H	Y	B	U	I	Z	J	F	E	P	C	E	N	A
13	S	E	E	D	C	C	N	D	N	E	I	R	F	Y	C	R
14	R	H	V	L	E	L	X	T	R	H	I	O	W	L	P	B
15	M	D	Q	R	K	O	D	X	D	O	C	T	O	R	W	I
16	O	I	T	G	R	A	N	D	P	A	W	J	O	N	V	L

Word Search Answer/Hints
The words below are listed with their starting row and column.

FAMILY MEMBERS
AUNT 11:5

BROTHER 8:10

COUSIN 10:15

FATHER 12:10

GRANDMA 7:4

GRANDPA 16:4

MOTHER 1:3

SISTER 2:11

UNCLE 8:1

OTHERS
COACH 10:7

DENTIST 5:13

DOCTOR 15:9

FRIEND 13:13

LIBRARIAN 16:16

NURSE 2:6

POLICE OFFICER 3:16

PRINCIPAL 12:12

TEACHER 8:7

Sounds the Same! Different Meanings!

Underline the letter in front of each correct answer.

1. It was a very cloudy ___.
  G. knight
  <u>H.</u> night

2. The ___ was hired to clean the room.
  N. made
  <u>O.</u> maid

3. There is a ___ in the shoelace.
  L. not
  <u>M.</u> knot

4. Kelly dressed as a ___ for Halloween.
  <u>O.</u> witch
  P. which

5. I ___ the song of the ice cream truck.
  O. here
  <u>P.</u> hear

6. Jennifer ___ her tennis match.
  G. one
  <u>H.</u> won

7. Dave ate a ___ for dessert.
  <u>O.</u> pear
  P. pair

8. My mother bought two dresses at the ___.
  M. sail
  <u>N.</u> sale

9. The ___ was good for playing baseball.
  <u>E.</u> weather
  F. whether

10. Sara is going on vacation next ___.
  <u>S.</u> week
  T. weak

These sets of words are **HOMOPHONES**. Like other homonyms, homophones also sound alike and have different meanings, but they also have different spellings.

39   Language Arts Crossword Puzzles: Grades 1–4

Hidden Pets

Find the pet hiding in each sentence.

1. If I **sh**are my chips, will you share your cookies? **fish**

2. They **do g**ood work when they try. **dog**

3. Stand u**p on y**our toes. **pony**

4. Eri**c at**e three pieces of pie. **cat**

5. Sam asked i**f Rog**er wanted to come to his party. **frog**

6. I ate **ham, Ster**ling ate chicken, and Seth ate pork. **hamster**

7. The teacher explained to Ki**p, "Ig**neous rocks include obsidian and basalt." **pig**

8. Kee**p up** the good work. **pup**

Optional Lists of Words and Terms

These lists are provided for your convenience should you choose to use them.

Synonyms

also	angry	close	correct	damp	fast	father
filthy	gift	glad	laugh	rich	sick	similar
small	start	story	tired	under	wicked	yelled

Antonyms

angry	buy	dark	early	exit	fix	found
hates	messy	never	outside	over	polite	pull
quietly	slowly	starting	wet	wide	won	young

Parts of Speech

adjective	adverb	articles	common	conjunction
interjection	noun	ouch	plural	preposition	pronoun	proper
quickly	read	red	singular	they	to	verb	we

Rhyming Words

bear	cries	dawn	dollar	done	funny	gift
kept	law	lies	mouse	near	past	paint	sail
scream	shore	soil	thick	toss	true	zoo

Nouns: At School

bell	books	bus	chairs	chalk	class	desk	dictionary	erase
food	gym	homework	librarian	map	math	nurse	paper
pen	pencil	principal	quiz	science	students	teacher	test

Nouns: At Home

bed	blanket	bowl	chairs	clock	couch	door
family	food	fork	garage	iron	kitchen	knife
lamp	pet	pillow	rug	sink	table	toaster	TV

Pronouns

he   her   hers   him   I   it   me

mine   our   she   that   their   theirs   them

these   this   those   we   yours

Verbs

adopted   are going   arranged   ate   call   came   did

drank   drinks   eats   fell   forgot   found   has

knew   ran   read   rode   said   saw   sit

sits   sleep   thought   went   wil   eat

Adjectives

angrier   bad   beautiful   better   bright   calm   cold

damp   different   dry   graceful   happiest   loud   luckier

nervous   softer   thickest   warmest   weak

Adverbs

almost   always   angrily   badly   bravely   carefully

clearly   eagerly   early   finally   happily   loudly

magically   never   nicely   patiently   politely   quietly

really   safely   since   sometimes   tomorrow

www.ingramcontent.com/pod-product-compliance
Lightning Source LLC
Chambersburg PA
CBHW081305040426
42452CB00014B/2652